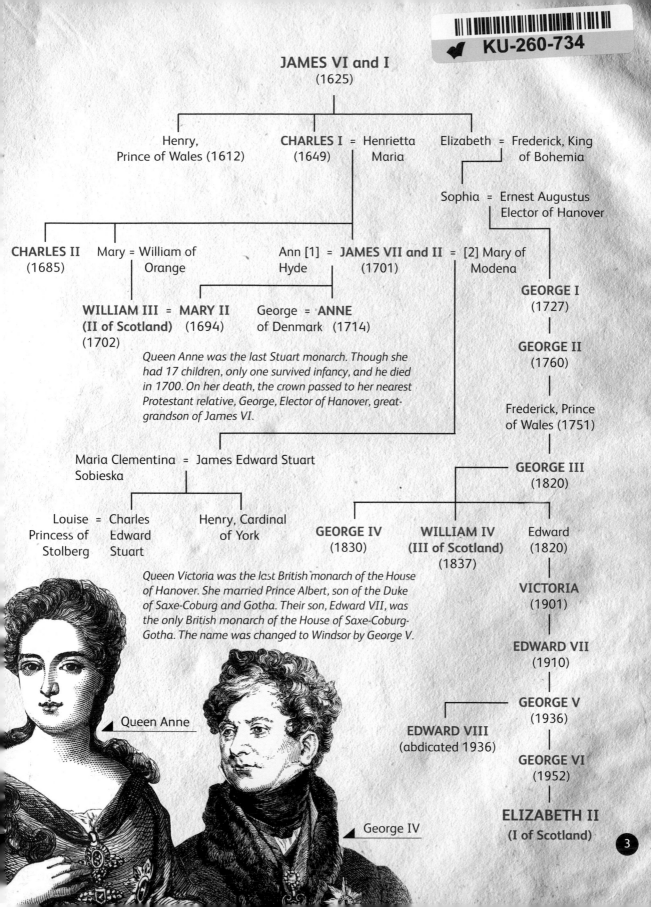

JAMES VI and I
(1625)

Henry,
Prince of Wales (1612)

CHARLES I = Henrietta
(1649)   Maria

Elizabeth = Frederick, King
            of Bohemia

Sophia = Ernest Augustus
         Elector of Hanover

CHARLES II
(1685)

Mary = William of
       Orange

Ann [1] = **JAMES VII and II** = [2] Mary of
Hyde   (1701)   Modena

GEORGE I
(1727)

WILLIAM III = **MARY II**   George = **ANNE**
(II of Scotland) (1694)   of Denmark (1714)
(1702)

GEORGE II
(1760)

*Queen Anne was the last Stuart monarch. Though she
had 17 children, only one survived infancy, and he died
in 1700. On her death, the crown passed to her nearest
Protestant relative, George, Elector of Hanover, great-
grandson of James VI.*

Frederick, Prince
of Wales (1751)

Maria Clementina = James Edward Stuart
Sobieska

GEORGE III
(1820)

Louise = Charles
Princess of Edward
Stolberg   Stuart

Henry, Cardinal
of York

GEORGE IV
(1830)

WILLIAM IV
(III of Scotland)
(1837)

Edward
(1820)

*Queen Victoria was the last British monarch of the House
of Hanover. She married Prince Albert, son of the Duke
of Saxe-Coburg and Gotha. Their son, Edward VII, was
the only British monarch of the House of Saxe-Coburg-
Gotha. The name was changed to Windsor by George V.*

VICTORIA
(1901)

EDWARD VII
(1910)

▶ Queen Anne

GEORGE V
(1936)

EDWARD VIII
(abdicated 1936)

GEORGE VI
(1952)

▶ George IV

ELIZABETH II
(I of Scotland)

3

What is a Jacobite?

Jewellery bearing a portrait of King Charles II. Such jewels were, to their owners, much like keepsakes or photographs today.

Where did the name 'Jacobite' come from? What were the Jacobites fighting for, and why?

It all began in 1676, when James, Duke of York, brother of Charles II, officially became a Roman Catholic. When he succeeded to the throne as James VII of Scotland and II of England and Ireland in 1685, he declared that everyone was now free to practise their own religion. Protestants, however, saw this as a step towards making Catholicism the national religion. In 1688 James' second wife, the Catholic Mary of Modena, had a son, James Francis Edward Stuart, who was now heir to the throne.

Protestants in England asked the Dutch Protestant Prince William of Orange, James' nephew, to come over to Britain with an army to make James see their point of view. When James panicked and fled to France, William was invited to become king in his place, sharing the throne with his wife Mary, daughter of James.

Some still regarded James as their rightful king, and his son as heir to the throne. These people called themselves Jacobites (*Jacobus* is Latin for James). Even if James had lost the crown, this did not immediately apply to his son.

There were many Jacobites in Scotland, where the Stuart family had ruled for over 300 years since Robert II became King of Scots in 1371.

After the death in 1701 of James VII, the hopes of the Jacobites rested on his son (left), whom they regarded as James VIII and III.

Others later called him the 'Old Pretender'. His son, Charles Edward Stuart (right, aged about 11), became known as the 'Young Pretender'.

4

National Museums Scotland

The Jacobites

Antony Kamm

SCOTTIES SERIES EDITORS
Frances and Gordon Jarvie

Contents

Original edition published in 1995
by HMSO publications

Published from 2000 by
NMS Enterprises Limited – Publishing
a division of NMS Enterprises Limited
National Museums Scotland
Chambers Street, Edinburgh EH1 1JF

Revised and reformatted edition 2009

Text © Antony Kamm 1995, 2009
Images (© below and activities section p. viii)

ISBN: 978-1-905267-28-6

British Library Cataloguing in Publication Data
A catalogue record of this book
is available from the British Library.

Book design concept by Redpath.
Cover design by Mark Blackadder.
Layout by NMSE – Publishing.
Printed and bound in the United Kingdom by
Henry Ling Ltd, Dorchester, Dorset.

CREDITS

*Thanks are due to the individuals and organisations
who supplied images and photographs.*
*Every attempt has been made to contact copy-
right holders to use the material in this publication.
If any image has been inadvertently missed, please
contact the publisher.*

NATIONAL MUSEUMS SCOTLAND
(© The Trustees of National Museums Scotland)
for illustrations used on front and back cover
(print 1797 [Laurie & Whittle, publisher]), with
locket of Charles Edward Stuart;
for illustrations on pages 4 (Charles II jewellery);
7 (pistol, dirk, Highlander figures, sporran, brooch);
10 (Blair Castle, SLA); 13 (Glencoe, SLA); 15 (Earl
of Mar); 16 (dirk, sword, targe and pistol); 18
(medal); 19 (Wade map); 20 (Rob Roy MacGregor);
21 (exploding sporran); 24 (George II enamel);
26 (cutlery canteen and Prestonpans battle plan),
27 (Holyroodhouse); 28 (Captain Hugh Fraser);
29 (Duke of Cumberland and bayonet); 30
(Chisholm insignia); 31 (Ernest Grizet etching
after David Morier painting of Culloden from
Children of the Mist by Lord Archibald Campbell
[Edinburgh & London, 1890]); 31 (Barrel's regimental standard); 32 (Appin regimental standard,
cutlery canteen and pistol); 33 (Culloden battle
plan and Black Watch infantryman); 34 (Jacobite
glass); 38-39 (tartan and tartan ledger); activities
section pages i (Rob Roy MacGregor); iv and v
(details from 'Highlanders at Mayence 1743');
vii (piper and Highland woman)

**Further credits at the end of the activities
section (p. viii).**

For a full listing of NMS Enterprises
Limited – Publishing titles and related
merchandise:
www.nms.ac.uk/books

Genealogical chart

ROBERT I, the Bruce
(1329)

DAVID II
(1371)

Marjorie = Walter the Steward

ROBERT II
(1390)

ROBERT III
(1406)

JAMES I
(1437)

JAMES II
(1460)

JAMES III
(1488)

■ Kings and queens of Scotland from Robert I

■ Kings and queens of England from Henry VII

■ Kings and queens of Scotland and England from James VI and I

(Dates indicate year of death)

The marriage in 1503 between James IV and Margaret Tudor, daughter of Henry VII of England, led to their great-grandson, James VI, becoming King of England as well as Scotland.

HENRY VII
(1509)

JAMES IV [1] = Margaret = [2] Archibald
(1513)   Tudor   Douglas

HENRY VIII
(1547)

JAMES V
(1542)

MARY   **ELIZABETH**   **EDWARD VI**
(1558)   (1603)   (1553)

Lady Margaret = Matthew Stuart
Douglas   Earl of Lennox

MARY
Queen of Scots
(abdicated 1567)

= Henry Stuart, Lord Darnley

James VI and I →

JAMES VI and I
(1625)

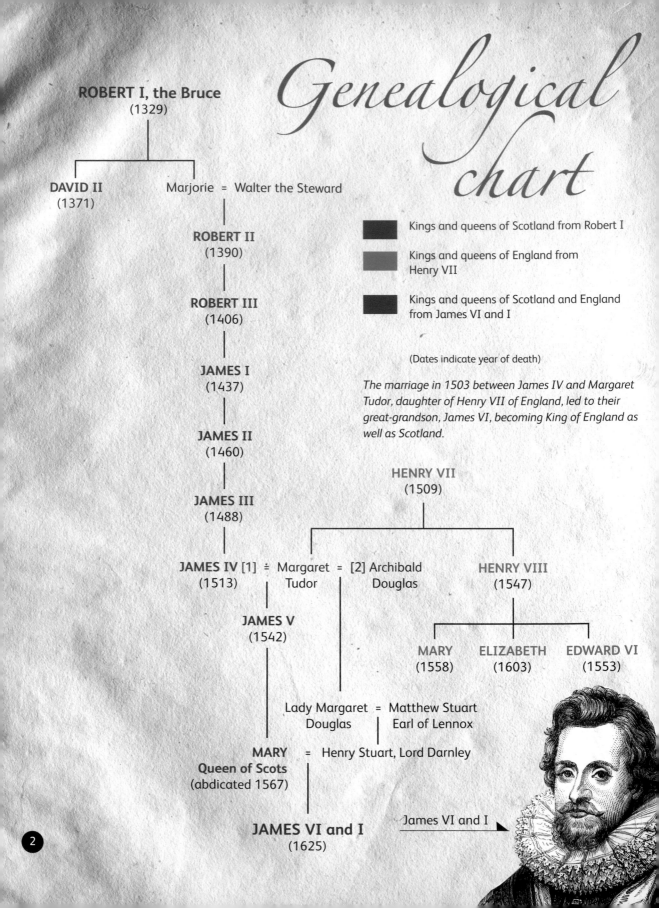

What's in a name?

King Robert II's father was Walter, High Steward (or Stewart) of Scotland. The Scottish royal family adopted the spelling Stuart in the time of Mary, Queen of Scots, who was brought up in France. There is no 'w' in the French alphabet.

Scottish Jacobites had other grievances. In 1690, by order of the Scottish Parliament, the Episcopal Church was finally replaced by Presbyterianism as the official faith in Scotland. Both Catholics and Episcopalians disliked Presbyterianism being the national religion, and strongly resented methods used to enforce it. Jacobites, like most other Scots, also objected to the union of the English and Scottish parliaments in 1707.

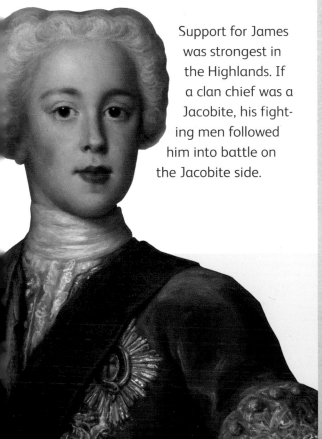

Support for James was strongest in the Highlands. If a clan chief was a Jacobite, his fighting men followed him into battle on the Jacobite side.

Genealogy

If you look at the genealogical chart on pages 2-3, the mother of William III was the sister of Charles II and James VII. William's wife Mary was the daughter of James VII. Both William and his wife were thus grandchildren of Charles I.

The Episcopal Church of Scotland

Episcopalians uphold Church rule by bishops, and regard the reigning king or queen as head of their Church. Presbyterians believe in Church rule by elders and ministers. In parts of northern Scotland at the time of the union of parliaments, almost half the population was Episcopalian.

Highland life and customs

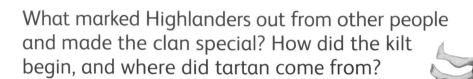

What marked Highlanders out from other people and made the clan special? How did the kilt begin, and where did tartan come from?

Highlanders spoke their own language – Gaelic. They lived according to their own customs. They had their own music (harp and the pipes) and their own distinctive dress. Clan councils took decisions and made laws for their own people.

Clann in Gaelic means 'children', and all members of a Highland clan are supposed to be descended from the same ancestor, whose name they bear. The hereditary clan chief occupied his lands by law, but he also had to defend them from attacks by other clans.

Plaid

To get into the plaid, you laid it on the ground with the belt underneath, and arranged it in pleats lengthwise. Then you lay down on it and gathered the bottom part round your waist, securing it with the belt. There were several ways of draping the top part round and over your body. At night, out in the open, the plaid became a sleeping bag.

Local justice

The clan chief upheld the laws of his clan and of his government, and had the power to judge and to punish those who transgressed. This tradition, known as heritable jurisdiction, was highly prized throughout Scotland by those who exercised it: chiefs, sheriffs, landowners, and barons (those who held land from the Crown).

The basic Highland garment was the plaid, whose Gaelic name, *Feileadh Mór* (Big Wrap), describes it perfectly. This enormous, midge-proof, tartan blanket was woven from wool brightly-coloured with vegetable dyes. Tartan, which is not a Highland word, means 'patterned with stripes of different colours crossing each other at right angles'. There were no special clan tartans until the 19th century.

The kilt, or *Feileadh Beag* (Little Wrap), is said to have been invented in about 1720 by the English manager of an ironworks in Glengarry. More likely, it reflected a natural development, which began in the 18th century in the army, of the belted plaid to the shorter kilt.

When armed, a Highlander carried his targe (shield), dirk (sometimes with his knife and fork in the sheath), and sword.

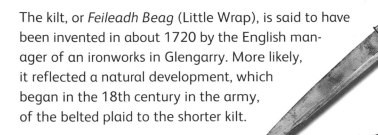

Well-dressed Highlanders

Arisaid, a checked plaid with a white background. Until about 1740, it was worn like a dress, with a belt, and a large brooch at the breast (see below, right). Later, it became an accessory – a long, oblong shawl which could be drawn over the head, or secured at the right shoulder with a circular brooch and draped over the body.

Those who could afford them might also have a pair of steel pistols and a musket, with a powder horn (often richly decorated) and ammunition pouch.

A sporran was useful for keeping valuables in, and, on active service, it also held a daily ration of oatmeal.

Out of doors, especially on the boggy moors, both men and women went bare legged and wore brogues. These were light shoes made of deerskin, with holes punched in them to let the water out.

Clan plant badge

Bonnet

Brooch

Tartan plaid

Long linen shirt

Short jacket

Sporran

Detail of a 17th-century brass Highland brooch, 17.5 cm in diameter, used to fasten the arisaid.

Garters, one metre long, tied on the outside with a special knot.

Tartan stockings

Buckled shoes

'Bonnie Dundee'

Each on behalf of their king, two armies and two generals prepare to fight it out!

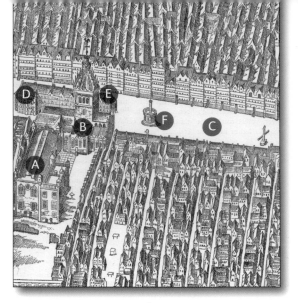

Detail of a 17th-century picture map of the High Street of Edinburgh.

KEY:
A – Parliament House
B – St Giles' Church
C – High Street
D – Tolbooth
E – Luckenbooths (shops with flats above)
F – Mercat Cross

In March 1689 a convention (assembly) met in Parliament House, Edinburgh, to hear letters from both William III and James VII asking for support. After these had been read out, even the keenest of James' supporters realised that his cause was hopeless and that William was about to be declared King of Scotland as well as of England.

Not so John Graham of Claverhouse, Viscount Dundee, a staunch Episcopalian and James' general in Scotland. He stormed out of the chamber and led his troop of cavalry into the High Street. They clattered

through the Netherbow Port (see page 25), turned left down Leith Wynd, and entered the suburbs below Calton Hill. Then they rode along the farther shore of the North (Nor') Loch (now Princes Street Gardens), rounded its western edge and halted below the Castle Rock. The Castle, commanded by the Catholic Duke of Gordon, was besieged by supporters of William. Dundee climbed up the west face of the rock to encourage Gordon to hold out as long as he could.

Then Dundee rode out to rally an army of the clans to fight for James against the Government of William and Mary. He raised the royal standard of James VII on the heights of Dundee Law. He sent out letters calling for a gathering of the clans beside the river Spean. There he recruited an army of

Twenty years earlier, Claverhouse (left) had served under King William, then Prince William of Orange, in the Dutch wars against France. It is said that he saved William's life in battle.

about 2000 men, under their chiefs, among them the legendary Cameron of Lochiel.

Most of Dundee's army had never fought in a proper battle before, but he trained his Highlanders in the latest fighting methods. He ate with his men, and slept alongside them on the ground. He was their hero, even when he would not let them take plunder. The Government offered a large reward for Dundee's capture, dead or alive, but no one gave him away.

Against him, William and Mary sent a Scot, General Mackay, with the best available troops. For several weeks the two armies avoided each other. On 26 July, after a four-day march from the west, Dundee's Highlanders, tired and hungry, reached Blair Castle. Blair Castle was vital to both sides. Whoever held it controlled the main route to the north, through the long, narrow Pass of Killiecrankie.

Mackay was in the south with an army of 3000, including three regiments of regular soldiers, when he heard Dundee was on the move. He came north against him. On the evening of 26 July, Mackay camped at the entrance to the Pass.

Viscount Dundee was still five miles away. Should he march at dawn with his exhausted, untried troops, and catch Mackay's army as it emerged from the Pass? Or allow Mackay to go through, and then hope to defeat him by force of numbers when the extra men he was expecting from more distant clans had arrived? Dundee held a council of war. After much discussion on both sides, he invited Lochiel to have the last word.

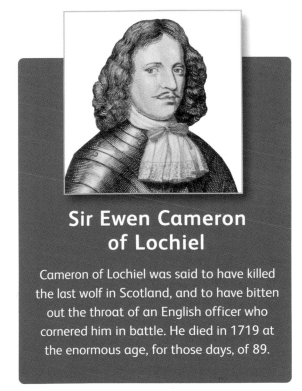

Sir Ewen Cameron of Lochiel

Cameron of Lochiel was said to have killed the last wolf in Scotland, and to have bitten out the throat of an English officer who cornered him in battle. He died in 1719 at the enormous age, for those days, of 89.

This drawing of Edinburgh from the north west was made in about 1690 by John Slezer. Dundee's route can be followed. Clambering up the rock was an extraordinary feat for a man of forty.

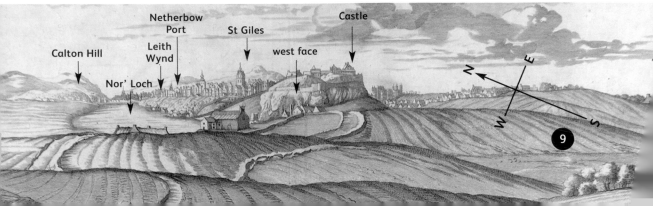

Calton Hill · Nor' Loch · Leith Wynd · Netherbow Port · St Giles · west face · Castle

The Battle of Killiecrankie
27 July 1689

Opposite page: Modern painting of the rout. In battle, Highlanders threw off their plaids and fought in their shirts, with the tails tied between their legs. At Killiecrankie, Cameron of Lochiel, seeing his men were barefooted, took off his own boots and threw them aside.

Above: Blair Castle. The oldest part dates from 1269, but in the 1740s the castle was converted into a comfortable country mansion. The castellations and turrets were reinstated in the 1870s.

The decision is made, but what was the outcome of the battle, and what happened next?

Cameron of Lochiel was all for fighting at once. Dundee led out his army, not along the road, but through the glens behind Blair Castle. There they halted on the hillside over-looking the exit to the Pass.

When the government soldiers came out of the Pass, there was no opposition in front of them. Then they saw a few Highlanders high up to their right. Mackay gave orders to right turn and advance up the hill. At the top of the slope, the ground flattened out. Beyond was another rise.

On the crest of the second rise was the whole Jacobite army, drawn up clan by clan in battle formation. In the line, with his small troop of faithful horsemen, was Viscount Dundee. He had been persuaded to change his usual red coat for one of yellow-brown, so that he would be less conspicuous.

For two hours, while Mackay organised his troops as best he could, and the sun dropped slowly towards the top of the hill across the valley, Dundee kept his wild Highlanders in check. Then, when the sun was no longer in their faces, he gave the order to charge.

The government troops fired off their muskets and then struggled to fit bayonets into the muzzles. Highlanders with guns obeyed orders and waited to fire until they were so close that they could not miss. Then they drew their fearsome, double-edged broadswords. The rest charged with them. Mackay's lines disintegrated. The fight was over in three minutes.

MacKay had lost the battle, but not the campaign. At the moment of victory,

Dundee was killed by a stray bullet. Without his leadership, the clans were defeated shortly afterwards in a street battle in Dunkeld. The first Jacobite rising had collapsed.

This was not the end of Jacobite hopes in Scotland, especially as King William was proving to be unpopular. Many clan chiefs still regarded James VII as their king. William preferred to fight a war in France than secure his position in Scotland. Some other way had to be found to subdue the Highlands.

In August 1691 a royal proclamation was issued offering an amnesty to clan chiefs who swore an oath of allegiance to William and Mary. One powerful man in London did not believe that this was enough. He was Sir John Dalrymple, known as the Master of Stair. He was also Secretary of State for Scotland, and he was devising a wicked plot.

Dalrymple (below) had been in trouble in 1682, when he was convicted of obstructing Claverhouse in his duties as Charles II's representative in Galloway.

Royal Proclamation

'We are resolved Graciously to Pardon, Indemnifie, and Forgive all that have been in Arms against Us or Our Government [who shall] Swear and Sign the Oath of Allegiance to Us [by] the first day of January next. ... Such as shall still continue obstinate, and incorrigible, after this Gracious offer of Mercy, shall be punished as Traitors and Rebels.

'GOD save King William and Queen Mary'

The Massacre of Glencoe

A most shameful episode, but who was ultimately to blame?

Jacobite chiefs wanted permission from James VII before they took the oath of allegiance. James did not make up his mind until 12 December 1691, when he wrote a letter to his military commander in Scotland authorising his 'loyal subjects' to do what was best for their own safety. When the letter arrived in Edinburgh, little time was left for distant clans to take the oath before the deadline.

Alasdair MacDonald of Glencoe waited until the last minute before, on 31 December, reporting to the military governor at Fort William. He was told that only a sheriff could administer the oath. The nearest was at Inveraray, some 70 miles away through driving snow. MacDonald arrived there on 3 January, but the sheriff was on holiday.

MacDonald finally took the oath on 6 January. He apologised for being late, and begged the sheriff to put in a good word for him. The sheriff promised to do this.

On 2 February 1692, two officers and 120 men, under the command of Campbell of

From the Report of the Official Enquiry
June 1695

'Secretary Stair, in a letter dated 3 December [1691], states that the government is obliged to ruin some of the Highlanders to weaken and frighten the rest, and that the Macdonalds will fall into this net. A month before the expiry of the King's indemnity, he seems to be planning that some of them should be rooted out and destroyed.'

Glenlyon, arrived at Glencoe and demanded to be billeted there. Under the rules of Highland hospitality, they were made welcome. Members of the clan entertained them, and gave them beds, food, and drink.

At 5 a.m. on the morning of 13 February the killing began. Some of the MacDonald clan were away, but 38 men, women, and children were shot and bayoneted that day.

The Government tried to cover up the scandal. It was, however, a publicity opportunity for the Jacobites. They leaked the news to the *Paris Gazette*, copies of which reached

Opposite page (left-hand column): extracts from Stair's letters written in January 1692; (right-hand column): extract from the orders to Campbell of Glenlyon to massacre his hosts, with (below) the original document in full, signed by Robert Duncanson.

London on 12 April. Everyone now knew about the massacre at Glencoe. Yet nothing happened for three years!

Finally, in 1695 King William was persuaded that there must be an official enquiry. As a result of the commission's report (see extract opposite), the Scottish Parliament, in an address to the King, concluded that Stair had 'exceeded your Majesty's instructions'. The lesser actors, who 'barbarously killed men under trust', should be prosecuted and the survivors of the slaughter compensated.

Nobody was ever brought to court. Stair resigned his offices of state, but received the King's pardon for anything he had done and was awarded an extra pension.

From Secretary Stair's letters to Commanding Officer, Scotland

11 January 1692

'My Lord Argyll tells me that Glencoe has not taken the oath, at which I rejoice. It is a great work to be industrious in rooting out that damnable sect, the worst in all the Highlands.'

16 January 1692

'The King is inclined to be merciful to those who were late, but, for a just example of vengeance, I entreat you to root out the thieving tribe of Glencoe.'

30 January 1692

'I am glad that Glencoe did not come within the prescribed time.'

To Campbell of Glenlyon from his superior officer

12 February 1692

'You are hereby ordered to fall upon the Rebels, the McDonalds of Glencoe, and to put all to the sword under seventy. ... [If you fail to do this] you may expect to be dealt with as one not true to King nor Government, nor a man fit to carry commissions in the King's service.'

SCENE OF THE MASSACRE OF GLENCOE 13TH FEBRUARY 1692.

'Bobbing John'
and the 1715 Rebellion

Why the Scots were upset, and why and how the Earl of Mar rebelled against King George.

After the death of Queen Mary in 1694, William ruled alone. He died in 1702 after being thrown from his horse when it stumbled over a mole-hill. Jacobites drank to the 'little gentleman in black velvet' – the mole who made the mole-hill. William was succeeded by Anne, Mary's sister.

Queen Anne had no children who survived. The English Parliament had decided that after her, the throne should go not to James Edward Stuart, her half-brother, but to George, her second cousin, the ruler of the Electorate of Hanover in Germany.

James was Catholic, like his father; George was a Lutheran Protestant. As the Scots were not even consulted about this, many of them felt that they were not bound by the decision.

When George I came to the throne, even some of the Scots who had previously supported the Government had become disillusioned. Among these was John Erskine, Earl of Mar. Although he was a Tory, he had worked hard for the Act of Union in 1707, when the Scottish and English parliaments were combined in London. George not only dismissed Mar from his post as Secretary of State for Scotland, but then snubbed him at a party.

George I. The government side in the battles that followed his accession was known as the Hanoverians, after the House of Hanover, to which George belonged.

The Earl of Mar

Mar was a smooth and resourceful politician, as well as a skilled architect and garden designer. His nickname was 'Bobbing John'. During his lifetime this probably referred to a physical disability which caused him to bob up and down. Afterwards, it came to describe his habit of changing sides, or even working for both sides at the same time.

In September 1715, at the family estate at Braemar, Mar raised the standard of James VIII (James Edward Stuart), before 600 Jacobite supporters. The flag, made of blue silk, had been lovingly stitched in gold by Mar's second wife, whom he had married the previous year. Although the gold ball at the top of the pole fell off, Mar ignored this bad omen and gave a rousing speech.

Mar had the support of some of the Scottish nobility, as well as many, but not all, of the clans. In November at Sheriffmuir he had an army of 7000 men. James Drummond, 2nd Duke of Perth, commanded his cavalry in the centre, with George Keith, Earl Marischal of Scotland, leading two squadrons of cavalry on the right flank. Opposing them on the government side was a professional soldier,

John Campbell, 2nd Duke of Argyll and chief of Clan Campbell, with 3000 men. With him was his brother, Archibald Campbell, a prominent Whig politician.

Below: The Duke of Argyll. His father successfully petitioned King William to appoint the future 2nd Duke colonel of the Argyll regiment when he was only 14 years old.

Genealogy

Look again at the genealogical chart on pages 2-3 to check George's claim to rule England and Scotland. He and Queen Anne were both great-grandchildren of James VI.

The Battle of Sheriffmuir

Highland targe, broadsword, dirk, and pistol.

13 November 1715

The battle was hard fought, but which side won?

It was an extraordinary battle, on a freezing day. The heathery moorland had so many humps and hollows that the two armies had difficulty finding each other. During the fighting, the two commanders, each on his own right wing, could not see what was happening elsewhere.

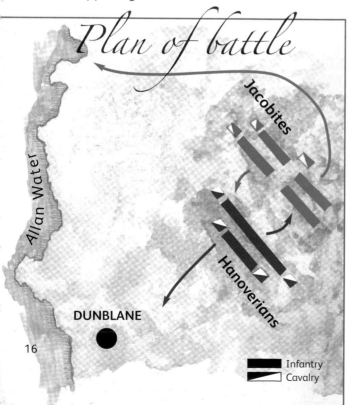

Plan of battle

Jacobites

Hanoverians

Allan Water

DUNBLANE

▬ Infantry
◤ Cavalry

Clan feuds

Long and bitter hostilities between clans were common. The most hated, because it was the strongest, was Clan Campbell. The Duke of Argyll was chief, or *MacCailein Mór*, of Clan Campbell. On the right of the Jacobite front line were the MacLeans, sworn enemies of the Campbells, and the MacDonalds of Glengarry and Glencoe. As the battle began, the chief of the MacLeans shouted, '*This is the day we have longed for. There stands MacCailein Mór for King George. Here stands MacLean for King James. Gentlemen, CHARGE!*'

The Highlanders behind him threw off their plaids, fired their muskets, and rushed forwards with their broadswords at the ready. When the Hanoverians fired back, and the Highlanders wavered, a MacDonald chief rallied them. Recalling that a Campbell commanded the troops who massacred the people of Glencoe, he cried, '*Revenge! Revenge! Today for revenge, and tomorrow for mourning!*'

When the fighting began, the infantry regiments on the Hanoverian left wing were still hurrying up the slope to the battlefield. The Highland clans on the Jacobite right wing made a furious charge and drove them back onto their own cavalry, causing great confusion. The retreat was sounded and the Hanoverian left wing fled. Mar and his Highlanders chased them as far as Dunblane.

Meanwhile, the Jacobite cavalry in the centre, under the command of the Duke of Perth, sat and waited for orders which never came.

The Jacobite left wing, which had no cavalry protection, was beaten back in a half circle to the Allan Water by Argyll's cavalry, with the help of the disciplined fire of his infantry. It was now dark. Each right wing had been victorious. The Jacobite survivors returned to Muthill, where they had camped the night before. The Hanoverians retired to Dunblane. In the morning Argyll led out his troops again, expecting to be overwhelmed by the superior numbers of the Jacobites.

What happened next? Argyll arrived on the battlefield with his depleted army. There was no opposition waiting for him. Mar had decided not to fight. When James Edward Stuart slipped into Scotland by sea in December, hoping to claim his kingdom, his chance had gone.

Right: James Drummond, whose father had been made 1st Duke of Perth by James VII in exile. The title was not recognised by the British Government. Earlier in the campaign of 1715 he had led a surprise attack on Edinburgh Castle, which failed.

How strong was your clan?

Here are the full fighting strengths at around this time of some of the clans in the Jacobite front line at Sheriffmuir:

MacLean 500 men
MacDonald of Glengarry 500
MacDonald of Glencoe 130
Macdonald of Sleat 700
MacDougall 200
Cameron 800
Stewart of Appin 300
McKinnon 200

The Campbells, however, could put 5000 fighting men into the field, though on that day Argyll's army only numbered about 3000.

The Rising of 1719

International skulduggery, a doomed enterprise, and an auspicious marriage.

By the Act of Grace in 1717, George I pardoned all those, with a few notable exceptions, who had been involved in Jacobite risings. The exceptions included the Earl of Mar and the Earl Marischal, who lost their titles and estates.

The Jacobite cause was not completely lost, however. Spain and Sweden were both keen to damage the power of England. Cardinal Alberoni, the Spanish chief minister, hatched a plot with the Irish-born Duke of Ormonde. Like Mar, Ormonde had become a Jacobite

Reverse of a medal struck to commemorate the Act of Grace. The figure, with a few unusual additions, is the Roman goddess Clementia, meaning mercy or compassion. The Latin inscription reads 'The mercy of Augustus', a reference to the Roman emperor Augustus, who regarded showing mercy to political enemies who rebelled against him as one of his special qualities.

after George I succeeded to the throne. The King of Sweden also promised arms and money, while the King of Spain provided ships and 5000 troops.

It was decided that at the same time as an invasion of England, a small expedition under the Earl Marischal would land in the west of Scotland and cause a diversion. But a storm scattered the invasion fleet, which never reached England. Though the Scottish

Secret agents

This is the opening paragraph of a letter written by Ormonde in Spain which was delivered in Rome on 26 January 1719. It is partly in code.

'To PETER
'14/a came to me privately and informed me that he had sent 21/1 to 507 to engage him to enter into an Alliance with 497, that the Chief Article was to endeavour to dethrone 249 their

common enemy, that he carryed Bills with him to enable 507 to make the attempt with promises of an Annual Subsidy provided he enter'd into the Allyance.'

PETER	=	James Edward Stuart
14/a	=	First minister of Spain
21/1	=	Spanish envoy in London
507	=	King of Sweden
497	=	King of Spain
249	=	George I

Marriage

James Edward Stuart was now 31. It was important that he should marry and have an heir. His advisers picked Maria Clementina Sobieska, a Polish princess. She was just 16 and very beautiful, the Pope was her god-father, she came with a dowry of valuable jewels, and she desperately wanted to be a queen. The marriage took place in Italy at midnight on 1 September 1719. On 31 December 1720, Maria had a son, Charles Edward Stuart.

expeditionary force of 250 Spaniards landed and was joined by 1000 Highlanders, it was doomed. The Jacobite arms store and garrison at Eilean Donan Castle were blown up by a government ship which had sailed into Loch Alsh. The land force fled from the engagement at Glenshiel in the face of mortar fire from a government army that included 130 Highlanders from clans which supported the Whigs.

That was the end of the 1719 rising. To try to prevent another one, the Government passed an act forbidding the carrying of arms. It was only partly successful. Whig clans gave up their weapons. Jacobite clans bought large quantities of broken and use-less weapons from Holland, which they delivered to the authorities, from whom they received compensation.

In 1724 the Government ordered General George Wade, a security expert, to produce a report on the position in the Highlands. He estimated that there were about 22,000 men able to bear arms. Of these, 10,000 supported the Government; the other 12,000 were Jacobites. In 1725 Wade was appointed commander of the forces in north Britain.

Wade's roads

Between 1726 and 1740 General Wade's soldiers built 243 miles of all-weather roads and 40 bridges for the movement of troops. In the background of this portrait mountains of the Highlands can be seen. A road squad is in action, with the tents of their camp in the glen behind.

Rob Roy MacGregor

Was Rob Roy a Jacobite, government spy, double agent, hero, thief, blackmailer, or all of these?

Rob Roy MacGregor, an engraving said to be 'from an original drawing'. In 1693 a law banning Clan MacGregor was included in a package of regulations intended to pacify the Highlands. All MacGregors had to change their names. Rob chose Campbell, after his mother.

Rob Roy is one of the most famous of all Highlanders. He was on the Jacobite side at the battle of Sheriffmuir, but he and other members of his clan appear to have arrived too late. He may, however, have been acting as a special agent for the Earl of Mar, or for the Duke of Argyll, or for both sides at once. In 1719 Rob Roy survived the Jacobite defeat at Glenshiel.

Rob Roy travelled hundreds of miles in Scotland and England to buy and sell cattle. It was common practice in Scotland to steal cattle, as well as to breed them and deal in them. Rob, however, had an extra way of making money. He invited rich landowners to pay him to protect their cattle from raiders. If they refused, he took their cattle himself!

As a Jacobite, Rob was hunted by Hanoverian troops. He was also pursued by the Government for cattle rustling and for helping poor people in trouble with the law

Whose side was he on?

Certainly Rob Roy behaved oddly at Sheriffmuir. John Cameron of Lochiel, chief of Clan Cameron, was with his clansmen in the front line of the Jacobite left wing, which was forced back to the Allan Water. Afterwards, he wrote to his clan:

'I rallied there all that I could find, and ordered those who had fired their muskets to reload them. At the same time I perceived Rob Roy MacGregor on his march towards me from Doune, he not being at the battle, with about 250 MacGregors and MacPhersons. I marched towards him with the few men I had got together. I entreated, he being with fresh men, that we should join up, cross the river, and attack Argyll, which he absolutely refused to do. I had such a small number when Rob Roy went off, and not knowing what had happened to our right wing, I could do nothing with so few.'

Exploding sporran

This unique 18th-century Highland sporran clasp (15.5 cm long, 10 cm high, and 4.5 cm deep) contains four miniature pistol barrels, each with its own chamber. These were capable of being fired should anyone tamper with the clasp or try to prise it open. Sir Walter Scott was so intrigued by it, that he wrote it into his novel, *Rob Roy* (1818), where the hero protects the contents of his sporran with a similar device.

or behind in their rents. He was hounded by the Duke of Montrose, to whom he owed money, and sought by the Duke of Atholl, who wanted the reward for capturing him.

Rob was caught several times, but always managed to escape. He finally died in his own bed. He was 63, a great age for someone then who spent most of his life out of doors in harsh weather, and who was for many years on the run.

His most daring escape was in 1717. He was tricked into meeting the Duke of Atholl, who captured him and sent him to Logierait Castle, the strongest prison in Perthshire. Three days later, he shared with his guards some whisky he had had sent in to him. Then he slipped away on a horse brought by his servant, who had arrived on the pretence of obtaining a message for Rob's family.

The unfortunate Atholl (right) had just written to General Carpenter, second-in-command of the Hanoverian forces in Scotland, praising himself for capturing Rob Roy. Now he had to write again.

The Duke of Atholl's apology

About an hour after I wrote to you yesterday, I had the misfortune to learn that Rob Roy had made his escape from the prison he was in at Logierait yesterday. …
I cannot express how vexed I am for this unlucky affair, but I assure you I shall leave no method untried that can be done to catch him. … I send you a copy of the orders I left for guarding him, which I did think was sufficient for one that had surrendered. … I have made the jailor prisoner, but nothing can retrieve this misfortune but apprehending him.

Atholl

21

Bonnie Prince Charlie

How the Prince came to Scotland, and how the '45 rising was launched.

On 23 July 1745, Charles, elder son of James Edward Stuart, landed in disguise on the tiny island of Eriskay in the Outer Hebrides. Without telling his father, he had borrowed money to hire a French warship, the *Elisabeth*, and 700 troops, and to buy arms and ammunition.

A frigate, the *Du Teillay*, carried Charles and 12 companions. When the *Elisabeth* was intercepted by a British man-of-war and so badly damaged that it had to turn back, Charles went on without it, to try to conquer Britain on his own.

'Action at Sea', painting by Harold Wylie. The *Elisabeth* (centre) is battling it out with the British man-of-war, HMS *Lion* (left), which was also badly damaged and had to return to port. The *Du Teillay* is on the right.

Two days later Charles was on the mainland, having landed on the shore of Loch nan Uamh. He immediately sent messages to clan chiefs who might support him. Some tried to persuade the Prince that the enterprise was so mad that he should return to Paris. He is reported to have replied:

'In a few days, with the few friends I have, I will erect the royal standard, and proclaim to the people of Britain that Charles Stuart is come over to claim the crown of his ancestors, to win it, or perish in the attempt. You may stay at home, if you prefer, and learn from the newspapers the fate of your prince.'

An engraving of Charles Edward Stuart. The Gaelic for Charles is *Theorlaich*, which, when spoken, sounds very like 'Charlie'.

That brave speech settled it. On 19 August, at Glenfinnan, before a gathering of 1300 supporters, the royal standard of the Stuarts was raised and Charles formally claimed for his father the thrones of Scotland, England, and Ireland. Alexander MacDonald, teacher and poet, who had been appointed as Charles' Gaelic tutor, spoke the words of a song which he had himself written. It began by stressing Charles' royal descent:

O Theorlaich mhic Sheumais, mhic
Sheumais, mhic Theorlaich
[*O Charles, son of James, son of*
James, son of Charles]

The great adventure had begun!

A cheeky challenge from Charles

The British Government offered a reward of £30,000 for Charles' capture. Charles responded by printing in Edinburgh a poster offering the same amount for the capture of the Elector of Hanover – that is, George II. Charles styles himself Prince of Wales, and also regent of Scotland, England, Ireland, and France. The French king eventually provided major funds for the expedition.

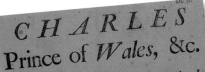

Help from the Highlands

The clans that joined Charles at the beginning of his campaign were MacDonald of Clanranald, MacDonald of Keppoch, MacDonald of Glencoe, MacDonald of Glengarry, Cameron of Lochiel, and Stewart of Appin. The first military success was scored by MacDonald of Keppoch. Eleven men yelling and a piper playing full blast ambushed two companies of the Royal Scots regiment. The government soldiers fled in panic and were afterwards taken prisoner by the rest of the clan.

Crests and mottos of the clans:
A. **MacDonald of Clanranald**
   ('My hope is constant in thee')
B. **MacDonald of Keppoch and of Glencoe**
   (Latin: 'By sea and by land')
C. **MacDonald of Glengarry**
   (Gaelic war cry: 'Raven's rock')
D. **Cameron of Lochiel** (Gaelic: 'Unite')
E. **Stewart of Appin** (Scots: 'Whither will ye')

The Jacobite Campaign

As the Jacobites march, General Cope has to catch up with them by sea.

George II in an oval enamel miniature, from a collection of Jacobite and other contemporary relics of Sir John Cotton, a prominent Tory politician whose father had played an active part in the 1715 rebellion.

Charles sent messages to other clans to join him on his way. Then he set out from Glenfinnan to secure his father's kingdoms. The very next day, General Cope, the Hanoverian commander in Scotland, advanced from Stirling to meet him.

They missed each other! The Jacobites marched on to Perth, where Charles made a triumphal entry into the city. Cope headed for Inverness, from where he led his men to Aberdeen to ship them to Dunbar.

George II, who had succeeded his father as king in 1727, now began to appreciate the real danger. He ordered ten infantry regiments to be brought home from Flanders.

With his army grown to nearly 2500, Charles continued his march. As he neared Edinburgh, Cope was embarking his army into ships at Aberdeen. When Charles made camp two miles outside the city walls to the south west, Cope's infantry and artillery were disembarking at Dunbar.

Lord George Murray

On the way, Charles was joined by Lord George Murray, a younger son of the Duke of Atholl who had been such a trial to Rob Roy. Murray, who, unlike Charles himself, was an experienced military man, was appointed a general. The other general was the Duke of Perth, eldest son of the Duke of Perth who had commanded the Earl of Mar's cavalry at Sheriffmuir.

Charles sent orders to Edinburgh's Town Council to surrender. The Council sent several deputations to the Prince by coach, hoping to prolong discussions until Cope arrived. Eight hundred Highlanders under Cameron of Lochiel waited outside the Netherbow Port for orders to storm the gate. In the end, they got in without a fight.

Cope prepared for battle at Prestonpans, in East Lothian. On the morning of 20 September, he drew up his army facing the direction from which the Jacobite force would come.

The Jacobites got into Edinburgh by trickery. The coach bringing the latest deputation back from Charles' camp dropped its passengers in the High Street. Then it continued its way to the Netherbow Port, to carry on to its stables in the Canongate. When the gate was opened, the Highlanders rushed through it from the outside. This drawing of the Netherbow Port from the High Street shows what it might have been like just after the incident.

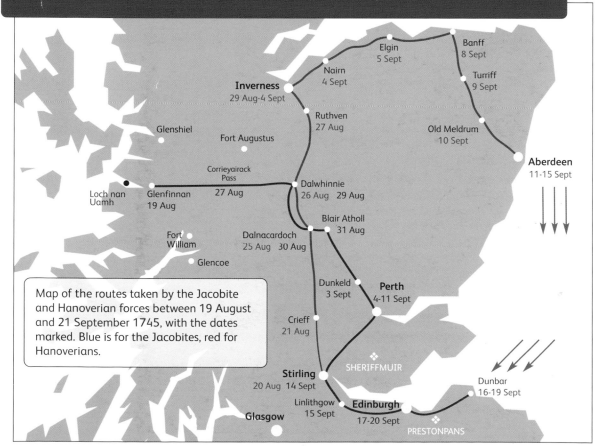

Map of the routes taken by the Jacobite and Hanoverian forces between 19 August and 21 September 1745, with the dates marked. Blue is for the Jacobites, red for Hanoverians.

Banff
8 Sept

Elgin
5 Sept

Nairn
4 Sept

Turriff
9 Sept

Inverness
29 Aug-4 Sept

Ruthven
27 Aug

Old Meldrum
10 Sept

Glenshiel

Fort Augustus

Aberdeen
11-15 Sept

Corrieyairack
Pass
27 Aug

Dalwhinnie
26 Aug   29 Aug

Loch nan
Uamh

Glenfinnan
19 Aug

Blair Atholl
31 Aug

Fort
William

Dalnacardoch
25 Aug   30 Aug

Glencoe

Dunkeld
3 Sept

Perth
4-11 Sept

Crieff
21 Aug

Stirling
20 Aug   14 Sept

SHERIFFMUIR

Dunbar
16-19 Sept

Linlithgow
15 Sept

Edinburgh
17-20 Sept

Glasgow

PRESTONPANS

Master of Scotland

John Cope's bad judgment, a glorious victory, and a shameful retreat.

Battle of Prestonpans

Prince Charles' silver and silver-gilt travelling canteen, containing cups, bowl, knives, forks, and spoons, cruet set, and corkscrew with nutmeg grater. It was only 15 cm high and weighed 1.14 kg, less than three cans of baked beans. To discover what eventually happened to it, see page 32.

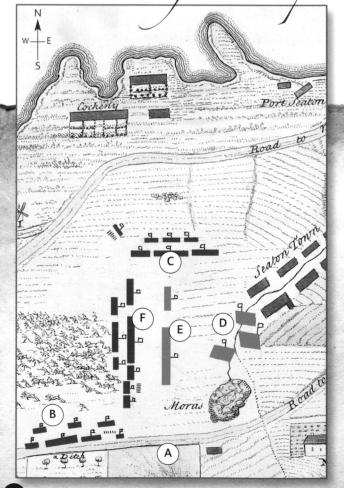

Left: Detail adapted from a battle plan of Prestonpans, published in 1745; Hanoverians are marked in red, Jacobites in blue. The Jacobites did not approach from the west, as Cope expected, but assembled on a hill [A] to the south of his position. Cope moved his troops to B, with marshy ground to his left, and then at about 3 p.m. retired to C, to await the attack.

The Jacobites, however, had been informed of a path through the marsh. Silently, during the night, they crossed it, and at about 5 a.m. the next morning mustered at D. When Cope realised they were there, he began to rearrange his lines at F, to face them. While he was still doing so, the Jacobites moved forward into battle formation E, and charged! The fight was all over in 15 minutes.

The Highlanders, some of whom were armed with scythes attached to poles, did terrible damage. Charles' military assistant wrote later: '*The field of battle presented a spectacle of horror, being covered with heads, legs, arms, and mutilated bodies.*'

General Cope escaped from the carnage and rode to Berwick, where it is said that he was sarcastically congratulated on being the first general to bring news of his own defeat!

Charles was generous to his opponents. He provided carriages to take the wounded from the battlefield and surgeons to dress their wounds. He later released the Hanoverian officers he had captured on condition that they promised not to fight against him again. After returning to Edinburgh, the Prince celebrated his triumph by dining in public at the Palace of Holyroodhouse, and holding a number of concerts and balls.

Charles was master of Scotland. Next on his list was the invasion of England.

An independent Scotland?

On 10 October 1745 Charles issued a declaration from Holyroodhouse, to the 'subjects of my Royal Father', calling for the abolition of the union of parliaments:

'*With respect to the pretended union of the two Nations, the King [James VIII] cannot possibly ratify it, since he has had repeated remonstrances against it from each Kingdom; and since it is incontestable, that the principal point then in view, was the exclusion of the Royal Family from their undoubted right to the Crown, for which purpose the grossest corruptions were openly used to bring it about.*'

Highlanders in the Canongate form a guard of honour in 1745 at the entrance to Holyroodhouse.

Contemporary
sketches

Sketches made at the time:

1. MacDonald of Glengarry.
2. Highlanders escorting a weeping woman. Is she a war widow? A thief? A government spy? No one knows.
3. Wounded Highlander.

Invasion of England

How Charles invaded England, and what happened next. The Hanoverians begin to get their act together.

The Jacobite army left Edinburgh on 1 November. That Charles and his Highlanders were able to march 200 miles into England unopposed was due to luck as well as good tactics. Though there was panic in London, and George II loaded his personal valuables on board a yacht ready to sail at a moment's notice, the luck could not last.

Hanoverian armies, under General Wade and the Duke of Cumberland (son of George II), finally managed to discover the Jacobite route. A third, much weaker, army was lined up to protect London itself. Charles had told his supporters that they could expect English Jacobites to join them and that France was mounting an invasion of southern England. Neither of these things happened, if indeed they were ever more than fancies. At Derby, 130 miles from London, he was persuaded to turn back. The long retreat had begun.

A call for funds by King George II

'Gentlemen of the House of Commons
I rely on your affection to me, and your care and concern for our common safety, to grant me such a supply as may enable me entirely to extinguish this rebellion, effectually to discourage any foreign power from assisting the rebels, and to restore the peace of the Kingdom; for which purpose I will order proper estimates to be laid before you. Amongst the many ill consequences of this wicked attempt, the extraordinary burden which it must bring upon my faithful subjects very sensibly affects me. But let those answer for it whose treason has occasioned it, and my people be convinced what they owe to those disturbers of our peace who are endeavouring to make this Kingdom a scene of blood and confusion.'

17 October 1745

Right: Captain Hugh Fraser, a Highland Scot, who fought on the government side at Prestonpans, Falkirk, and Culloden.

There was short-lived success for Charles at Falkirk, where a Hanoverian army was forced to attack uphill, in driving rain, against a storm-force wind. The retreat continued to Inverness, the last town in Scotland capable of being a Jacobite stronghold. Meanwhile, Cumberland, with the best available troops and artillery, had reached Aberdeen, where he trained his men to counter Highland fighting tactics. Confident in his own destiny, Charles prepared to do battle on the open moorland of Culloden.

Below: A Jacobite hussar, one of about 60 light cavalry raised by John Murray of Broughton, Charles' secretary. The hussars wore distinctive fur hats, and were armed with scimitars and pistols (in holsters in front of the saddle).

Prince William Augustus, Duke of Cumberland

To combat the Jacobite threat, Cumberland, commander of the British forces overseas, was recalled to Britain with six battalions of foot soldiers and nine squadrons of dragoons (mounted infantry). At Culloden he was just 25, four months younger than his opponent, Charles Edward Stuart. After being wounded in the leg in his first military action in 1742, Cumberland chose always to ride. His obesity, caused by his lack of exercise, contributed to his death at 44.

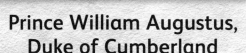

The Hanoverian army now had a bayonet, of a kind illustrated here. Instead of being plugged into the muzzle of the musket, which prevented it from being fired, the haft fitted round the mouth of the barrel. General Mackay had a similar idea after his experience at Killiecrankie, where the Highland charge had overrun his troops. He wrote in his memoirs, 'Having observed this method of the enemy, [I] invented the way to fasten the bayonet so to the muzzle without, by two rings, that the soldiers may safely keep their fire till they pour it into their breasts, and then have no other motion to make but to push as with a pike'. Cumberland also trained his soldiers, when facing a Highland charge, to thrust not at the man directly in front, but at the man to his left, whose right side would not be protected by his targe.

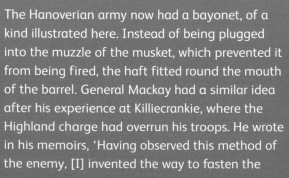

The Battle of Culloden

16 April 1746

Jacobite disaster. The battle and its grim aftermath.

The Jacobites were exhausted and hungry. Just one biscuit each had been issued during the previous 24 hours. When the battle began, Charles had only 5000 men: the rest were asleep or out looking for food.

Cumberland had 9000 disciplined troops. Many of his officers and men were Scottish: more Scots (including Highlanders) fought against Charles than for him during the rising of 1745/46.

Jacobite cannons began the battle. The superior Hanoverian artillery replied with devastating effect, driving great holes in the Jacobite lines as the men stood, with the wind, sleet, and snow in their faces, waiting for orders.

Loyalties

Motto: *Feros ferio*
(Latin: 'I frighten the fearsome')

One of the most poignant incidents of the battle relates to Clan Chisholm. The chief's youngest son, Roderick, leading the men of the clan in the left centre of the Jacobite front line [**10** on map, page 33], was killed early on by cannon fire. His two elder brothers, John and James, both captains in the Royals [**b** on map], were fighting opposite the Chisholms on the right of the Hanoverian front line. After the battle, they searched for Roderick's body, but could only find and bury what they thought was his, so mutilated was it.

The Highland charge, when it came, was chaotic. The centre went out ahead, but met boggy ground. The clans on the left, who had farthest to go, went last.

Culloden re-enactment 2007.

The Hanoverian gunners now switched from cannon balls to grapeshot (canvas bags stuffed with small projectiles) and canisters filled with musket balls, making their fire more deadly at short range.

Above: The wall of steel facing the Jacobite far right. An engraving of a painting done for Cumberland in 1746 by David Morier who is said to have used Jacobite prisoners and members of the Hanoverian regiment as models.

Below, left: The actual regimental standard, carried at Culloden, of Barrel's Regiment [**g** on map on p. 33], which bore the brunt of the Jacobite charge.

The Jacobite right now led the rest of the line. Jacobite infantry and cavalry from the second line [**EE** on map on p. 33] moved to cover the unexpected threat on their right flank from the Hanoverian dragoons [**DD** on map]. The Hanoverian infantry on the left of the front line poured musket fire into the charging Jacobites. Then they got stuck in with their bayonets! When the force of the charge caused the Hanoverian left to give way, reinforcements were immediately at hand to repel the attack and surround the Jacobite right wing. The Jacobite centre, and the left, never reached the Hanoverian lines at all.

As the disorganised retreat began, Charles was led from the field, and went into hiding.

His whole army was soon in flight, pursued by the Hanoverian infantry with fixed bayonets, harried by the Hanoverian cavalry from behind and from the side, and fired on by the Argylls on the flank. Wounded Jacobites were butchered where they lay. Many of those who were caught as they tried to escape were slaughtered. Others were to suffer unspeakable cruelties in Inverness jails, in churches converted into detention centres, and in prison ships moored nearby. The hunt was on for those who got away.

Charles' cutlery
(see page 26)

The travelling canteen (below) was packed with Charles' other luggage before the battle. When he was escorted off the field, he had to leave his baggage behind. The canteen was captured and presented to Cumberland, who gave it to one of his aides, in whose family it remained until 1963. It was acquired by National Museums Scotland in 1984.

Standard-bearer

Above: Regimental standard of the Stewarts of Appin, who fought on the Jacobite right wing [3 on map] under Stewart of Ardshiel. There is a legend about its survival. A wise woman prophesied that nine Donalds would fall bearing the blue banner. It was carried right into the Hanoverian lines by Donald Carmichael, standard-bearer to the Stewarts, who died in the hail of musket-shot and the grim bayonet thrusts. Seven more men called Donald, one after the other, struggled to raise the standard, only to be mown down. As the retreat began, Donald Livingstone, known as *Domhull Molach* (Hairy Donald), an 18-year-old friend of the Stewarts, ripped the flag from its staff, and wrapped it round his body. He was struck over the heart by a musket ball, but the folded silk acted as a bullet-proof vest. He escaped and, after numerous hair-raising exploits, returned the standard to its clan chief. He died at the age of 88.

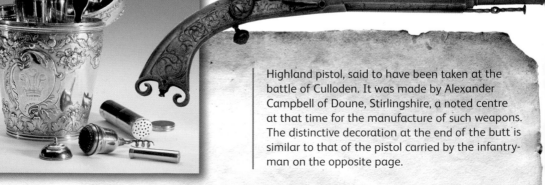

Highland pistol, said to have been taken at the battle of Culloden. It was made by Alexander Campbell of Doune, Stirlingshire, a noted centre at that time for the manufacture of such weapons. The distinctive decoration at the end of the butt is similar to that of the pistol carried by the infantry-man on the opposite page.

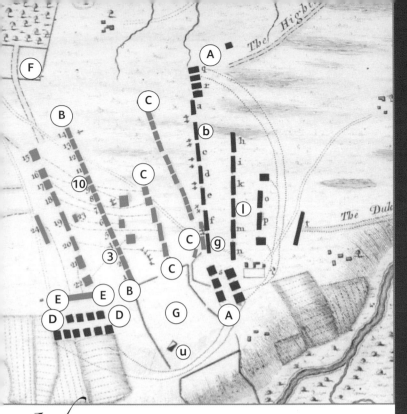

Detail from a map, dated 1746 and believed to have been drawn by John Finlayson, an Edinburgh instrument-maker who served in the Jacobite artillery at Culloden. It is a composite drawing, representing the situation at the beginning of the battle at 12 p.m. and about 50 minutes later as the Jacobite charge (blue) reaches the Hanoverian lines (red).

AA The position of the Hanoverian army when the battle began.

BB The Jacobite front line position when the battle began.

CC The Jacobite charge.

DD Ten half-squadrons of dragoons have ridden through the enclosure [G], whose walls have been broken down by men of the Argyll regiment [u], and now threaten the Jacobite right flank.

EE Jacobite infantry and a single squadron of cavalry move to oppose the Hanoverian dragoons.

F A single Jacobite artillery gun, which arrived late, has been manhandled into a corner of the enclosure on the Jacobite left. Its fire is so effective that eventually four Hanoverian guns and three mortars have to be run forward to take it out.

Infantryman

A Highland infantryman (1743) of the Black Watch, which fought as Sempill's Foot at Culloden in the left centre of the second Hanoverian line of battle [I on map].

Note the bonnet, rather than the cocked military hat, and the plaid, about 6 metres long and secured round the waist and at the left shoulder. The rod alongside the barrel of his musket is for pressing down the ball and charge.

He also carries his basket-hilted broadsword and, attached to his belt, ammunition pouch, dirk and bayonet. The pistol under his left arm hangs on a lanyard over his right shoulder. The musket, bayonet, and sword would be government issue.

The escape of the Prince

Charles is on the run. Where did he go, and how did he avoid being seen?

The Government hunted Charles by sea and by land for five months until he was taken off the west coast of Scotland by a French ship. He stayed only a few days in each place before moving on.

It is said that sometimes he got two or three others to impersonate him and take different routes, to confuse his enemies. He sailed to the Outer Hebrides, returning to the main-land by way of the island of Skye. He always managed to keep just ahead of his pursuers, though one by one his guides were arrested soon after delivering him to the next place of safety. The reward of £30,000 for his capture was still in force. No one ever betrayed him.

Sacrifice

One of Charles' impersonators was pursued and shot by troops. He kept up his heroic deception by exclaiming, as he fell, 'You have killed your prince!' The soldiers' mistake was discovered only when they produced the dead man's head at the next barracks to claim the reward.

Flora MacDonald

For two days Charles acted as Betty Burke, the Irish maid of 24 year-old Flora MacDonald. Flora took him from South Uist by boat to Skye, where she lived. Soon after parting from him, Flora was arrested. For assisting the Prince, she was briefly imprisoned in the Tower of London.

Betty Burke

Charles in disguise, as Betty Burke. Flora fell asleep during the sea passage to Skye. Charles, in his women's clothes, knelt across her with one hand on each side of her head, in case any of the men stumbled over her while attending to the sails.

OUTER HEBRIDES

LEWIS

Stornoway
5 May

Euirn (uninhabited)
7-10 May

Scalpa
30 April-3 May

Kingsburgh
29 June

Strathglass
4-8 Aug

✦ CULLODEN
16 April

Benbecula
27-29 April, 11-14 May,
24-28 June

Raasay
1-2 July

Loch
Cluanie
24-31 July

Fasnakyle
9-11 Aug

SOUTH
UIST

Portree
30 June

Glenshiel
22 July

Way
7-10 June

Glenmoriston

Corradale
15 May-5 June

Elgol 4 July

Glengarry
14 Aug

Fort
Augustus

Lochboisdale
15-20 June

Mallaig
5-7 July

Loch
Arkaig*

*Loch
Arkaig
dates
17 Apr,
16-20 Aug,
17 Sept

Eriskay

Borrodale
20-26 April, 10-16 July,
19 Sept

Loch nan Uamh

Glen Roy
14-15 Sept

Glenfinnan

Ben Alder
30 Aug-13 Sept

TO
FRANCE
(arrives 29 Sept)

> Map of the escape route of the Prince after Culloden: in red from 15 April to 27 June, in blue from 28 June to 29 September.

Final handshake?

One of the last people to say goodbye when Charles left the coast was Hugh Chisholm, a Highlander who had helped him. It is said that after shaking Charles' hand, Hugh would never give his right hand to anyone else. He broke this rule only once, with the daughter of his clan chief. He told her that she was the first and would certainly be the last to shake hands with him after the Prince.

Right: After the '45, Bishop Robert Forbes made an extensive collection of Jacobite documents relating to the rising, which he called *The Lyon in Mourning*. Inside the front cover of his third manuscript volume are personal mementos of Prince Charles: a piece of the ribbon on which he wore his Order of the Garter, a fragment of velvet from his sword hilt, and pieces of the dress, and of the string of the apron, that he wore as Betty Burke.

After the '45

Punishing measures by the Government, and their effects. What happened to Charles?

James Edward Stuart had settled in Italy, where he lived until his death in 1766. Charles was back in France. To ensure that there would be no further troubles, the British Government needed not only to punish the rebels, but to destroy the clan tradition. Various measures were introduced:

❖ The estates of 41 prominent nobles and chiefs were confiscated, and the incomes from these put to the general improvement of conditions in the Highlands.

❖ All heritable jurisdictions were abolished. From now on, all Scots were subject to the same system of justice.

❖ Also abolished was the custom, known as ward holding, whereby a tenant's allegiance to his chief included military service. Tenants were now free people, as long as they paid the rent.

❖ Not only was the carrying, or concealment, of arms again made a serious crime, but Highland dress was banned, except for the army.

Act for the Restraining of the Use of the Highland Dress

'From and after the first Day of August 1747, no Man or Boy within that part of Great Britain called Scotland other than such as shall be employed as Officers and Soldiers in His Majesty's Forces shall, on any pretence whatsoever, wear or put on the clothes commonly called Highland Clothes (that is to say) the Plaid, Philabeg or little kilt, Trowse, Shoulder Belts or any part whatever of what peculiarly belongs to the Highland garb; and that no Tartan or party-coloured Plaid or stuff shall be used for Great Coats or for Upper Coats; and if any such person shall presume after the first said day of August to wear or put on the aforesaid Garments or any part of them, every such person so offending shall suffer imprisonment without bail during the space of six months; and being convicted for a second offence shall be liable to be transported to any of His Majesty's Plantations beyond the Seas, there to remain for the Space of seven years.'

The new laws triggered off significant changes in Highland society. Throughout Scotland, however, opposition to the union of parliaments, one of the pillars of Jacobitism, remained strong for a time. Jacobite clubs continued to exist, their members toasting the Stuarts in glasses engraved with Jacobite emblems and mottos (see page 34). Catholic Ireland still hoped for self-government under a Stuart king. Scottish and Irish emigrants to north America and the Continent took their Jacobite sympathies with them.

Whatever happened to
Bonnie Prince Charlie?

Left: Charles in about 1748. He was still handsome, and still hoped to overthrow the kingdom of Britain. He now, however, fell out with the King of France, on whom the Jacobites depended for help.

Right, above: Charles at 34. Drink and a nomadic existence have begun to affect his looks. In 1750, thinking it would further his cause, he was received into the Church of England in London, in disguise. A British Government spy leaked information about a proposed Jacobite plot against George II in 1753, to coincide with a rising in Scotland, but the execution of Charles' emissary marked the end of Jacobite hopes in Britain.

Right: Charles in later years, a drunken, fat, ill-tempered old man. He married in 1772, at the age of 51. The French had promised him a large pension to produce an heir to embarrass the British Government.

and his partners and daughter

Charlotte Stuart (below) was Charles and Clementine's daughter, with whom he was reconciled in 1784. He made her Duchess of Albany, and died in her arms in 1788.

Princess Louise of Stolberg (above), Charles' wife, was 31 years younger than her husband. There was no heir. She had a series of affairs, and left him finally in 1780 for an Italian poet.

Clementine Walkinshaw (middle) met Charles in January 1746, when she nursed him through a bad cold while he was staying at her uncle's house at Bannockburn. In 1752, she joined him in his wanderings about Europe. Their daughter, born in 1753, was the only child he ever had. Because of Charles' abusive behaviour, Clementine left him in 1760, taking the child with her.

The Tartan Revolution

Mass emigration, and how the tartan was revived.

In the wake of the laws against the Highlands, clan chiefs became simply landlords. Many of them, who had spent all they had to help the Jacobite cause, were forced to sell their lands to sheep farmers from the south. Others, deprived of their private army which had brought them security and prestige, did the same.

The land had for many years been unable to support the Highland way of life. As the population grew, more and more people emigrated overseas. Many men joined the new Highland regiments raised to increase the fighting power of the British army abroad and to maintain the British empire.

To America

Between 1763 and 1775, 20,000 men, women, and children left the Highlands for north America alone. Among them were Flora MacDonald and her husband. They emigrated from Skye, where there was a dance called 'America'. The writer James Boswell, who visited the island in 1773 with Dr Johnson, described it: 'Each of the couples, after the common involutions and evolutions, successively whirls round in a circle, till all are in motion; and the dance seems intended to show how emigration catches, till a whole neighbourhood is set afloat.' Emigrants took with them not only their ways of life and their skills, but also the names of the places where they had been brought up.

General tartans

Black Watch

Scottish clans and many Scottish families have their own tartan or tartans. You are also entitled to wear a clan tartan if you belong to a sept (branch) of that clan. Those of Scottish descent who have no clan, family, or district tartan, may wear any of these four, though the Jacobite tartan is reserved for those who sympathise with the Jacobite cause:

Black Watch ❖ **Hunting Stewart Jacobite** ❖ **Caledonia**

There are seven places in USA called Aberdeen. One of them is in North Carolina, where there are also Bonnie Doune, Clyde, Glen Alpine, Hamilton, Highlands, Monroe, and Scotland Neck, and the counties of Alexander, Ladywell, Forsyth, Graham, Henderson, McDowell, Montgomery, and Scotland.

Tartans had in the meantime continued to be woven for the army. The repeal in 1782 of the act against Highland dress meant that tartan patterns could now be supplied also to civilians.

After the union of parliaments in 1707, the tartan began to be regarded as the Scottish distinctive dress. When it was allowed to be worn again it was proposed that each clan might have its own pattern.

The two ideas were finally realised in the most spectacular fashion in 1822, on the occasion of the state visit to Edinburgh of George IV. It was the first time a reigning monarch had visited Scotland for 171 years.

The celebrations were stage managed by Sir Walter Scott, who invited chiefs to bring their clansmen in Highland dress – many of them had to be kitted out with clan tartans

Above: A page from a ledger of tartan samples, collected by the Highland Society of London in the nineteenth century. The samples were endorsed and sealed by those who donated them

allocated to them by the suppliers. From this haphazard beginning developed the scientific study of tartans which prevails today.

George IV (seen in this cartoon) amused many, and delighted Walter Scott, by wearing full Highland dress, in the tartan which became known as Royal Stewart. In real life, the King did not suit the kilt as he was rather stout, his kilt was very short, and to cover the gaps between his kilt and his stockings, he wore pink tights. When someone commented on this at a reception at Holyroodhouse, Lady Saltoun, one of the guests, observed, 'We should take it very kind of him; since his stay will be so short, the more we see of him the better!'

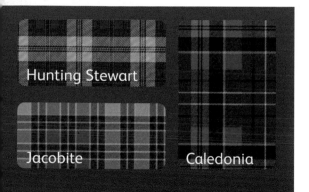

Hunting Stewart

Jacobite

Caledonia

PLACES OF INTEREST

Some of the places in Scotland with Jacobite associations. As opening times vary, it is advisable to check details on the internet or with a Tourist Information Centre.

VISITOR CENTRES

Clan Donald Centre (Museum of the Isles), Armadale, Skye
Culloden Centre, near Inverness
Glenfinnan Monument, Inverness-shire
Killiecrankie Centre, near Pitlochry
Skye Heritage Centre, Portree

MUSEUMS AND GALLERIES

Glencoe and North Lorn Folk Museum, Glencoe
Highland Folk Museum, Kingussie
Inverness Museum and Art Gallery
Kelvingrove Art Gallery and Museum, Glasgow
Montrose Museum
National Museums Scotland, Edinburgh
    National War Museum Scotland
    (situated at Edinburgh Castle)
Scottish National Portrait Gallery, Edinburgh
Stirling Smith Art Gallery and Museum
West Highland Museum, Fort William

CLAN AND TARTAN CENTRES

Clan Cameron Museum, Achnacarry
Clan Macpherson Museum, Newtonmore
Clan Tartan Centre, Leith Mills

CASTLES AND STATELY HOMES

Abbotsford House, Melrose
Alloa Tower
Blair Castle, near Pitlochry
Castle Fraser, Sauchen
Dunvegan Castle, Skye
Edinburgh Castle
Fort George, near Nairn
Fyvie Castle, near Turriff
Inveraray Castle
Palace of Holyroodhouse
Traquair House, near Peebles

RELATED WEBSITES (all accessed July 2009)

Battle of Culloden 1746
www.electricscotland.com/history/culloden

Battle of Prestonpans
www.battleofprestonpans1745.org/heritagetrust

British Battles
www.britishbattles.com

Culloden Centre
www.nts.org.uk/culloden

Historic Scotland
www.historic-scotland.gov.uk

The Jacobite Heritage
www.jacobite.ca

Jacobites – The 1745 Rebellion
www.bbc.co.uk/scotland/history/article/jacobites

The 1745 Rebellion
www.nottingham.ac.uk/mss/learning/conflict/theme2

The Lyon in Mourning
www.nls.uk/print/transcriptions
[From here you can access online versions of the volumes of *The Lyon in Mourning*, a collection of speeches, letters, journals, and other records of the times relating to Charles Edward Stuart, and also the day-by-day 'Itinerary of Prince Charles Edward Stuart', from his landing in Scotland in July 1745 to his departure in September 1746.]

The Massacre of Glencoe
www.amostcuriousmurder.com/Glencoe.htm

National Library of Scotland
www.nls.uk

National Museums Scotland
www.nms.ac.uk

National Trust for Scotland
www.nts.org.uk

The Northumbrian Jacobites
www.northumbrianjacobites.org.uk

Scottish History – Union and Rebellion
www.ltscotland.org.uk/scottishhistory/unionrebellion/index.asp

Scottish National Portrait Gallery
www.nationalgalleries.org

Scottish Tartans World Register
www.tartans.scotland.net/world_register.cfm.htm

Activities
Jacobites' Quiz

If you need help with any of the questions, you can look up the page or pages indicated.

1. Her Majesty Queen Elizabeth is descended from Robert the Bruce. True or false? (Pages 2-3)

2. King James V, as he was dying, was told that his queen had given birth to a daughter. Referring to the royal line of the Stewarts, he said, 'It came with a lass; it will go with a lass'. Who were the lasses, and was his prophecy true or false? (Pages 2-3, 14)

3. Jacobites believed that the rightful successor to James VII was (a) Charles II, (b) Charles Edward Stuart, (c) James Edward Stuart, (d) Queen Anne. (Pages 4, 14)

4. 'Heritable jurisdiction' means (a) a person's ancestral language, (b) powers of justice handed on by succession, (c) family landholdings, (d) inheritance tax. (Page 6)

5. At the time of the '45 rising, the clan tartan was a powerful influence in uniting bands of fighting men. True or false? (Pages 6, 39)

6. Many Scots (including Highlanders) fought against Charles Edward Stuart. True or false? (Page 30)

7. Which of these generals fought on the Jacobite side? (a) John Campbell, (b) John Cope, (c) John Erskine, (d) John Graham, (e) George Keith, (f) George Murray, (g) George Wade. (Pages 8-10, 14-17, 19, 24-27, 28)

8. Charles Edward Stuart publicly began his campaign in 1745 at (a) Glencoe, (b) Glenfinnan, (c) Glengarry, (d) Glengyle, (e) Glenshiel. (Pages 23, 25)

9. On 29 August 1745, the Jacobite army camped for the night at a place through which the government army had passed only two days before. It was (a) Dalnacardoch, (b) Dalwhinnie, (c) Dunbar, (d) Dundee, (e) Dunkeld. (Page 25)

10. The person most responsible for the Jacobite defeat at Culloden was Charles Edward Stuart. True or false? (Pages 30-32)

11. Fit these names to the faces:
    (a) Rob Roy MacGregor, (b) King George IV, (c) Cameron of Lochiel, (d) James Edward Stuart, (e) Charles Edward Stuart, (f) King William III.

Answers on page viii.

The original Rob Roy game

For two players.

You will need: a dice; two halma pieces or small tokens; eight pieces of card, about 7 cm by 8 cm.

You can either use the board on the opposite page, or photocopy it onto an A4 sheet, paste the sheet onto a piece of card, and, if you wish, colour in the shaded squares.

Chance cards
Write or print an instruction on each card:

(1) Safe Conduct
(2) Safe Conduct
(3) You make a profit at a cattle sale. Have another throw.
(4) Cattle disease. Miss a throw.
(5) Imprisoned in Logierait Castle. Play a Safe Conduct card or throw a six to escape.
(6) Take refuge in Glen Shira. Play a Safe Conduct card or throw an even number to proceed.
(7) Captured by Hanoverians. Play a Safe Conduct card or miss a throw.
(8) Successful raid on Montrose lands. Double your next score.

Shuffle the cards and place them in a pile face downwards.

The Rules
The winner is the first to arrive HOME by throwing the exact number.

After the instructions on a Chance Card have been carried out or a Safe Conduct played, the card is put on a 'used' pile. When there are no more cards in the chance pile, shuffle the 'used' pile and replace the cards face down.

Only one Safe Conduct card can be held at any time. If you pick a Safe Conduct card when you already hold one in your hand, you must discard it onto the 'used' pile. You are not bound to play a Safe Conduct card that is in your possession, but, if you do, you must play it before you throw the dice.

If you draw Logierait when you land on square 71, you cannot proceed until the turn after you have thrown a six.

If doubling your score takes you beyond HOME, then you move only the number of squares on the dice.

- HIGH WATER – Miss a throw.
- PASS OF ABERFOYLE and PASS OF BALQUHIDDER – Beware of ambush. Play a Safe Conduct card or throw a two or a three to proceed.

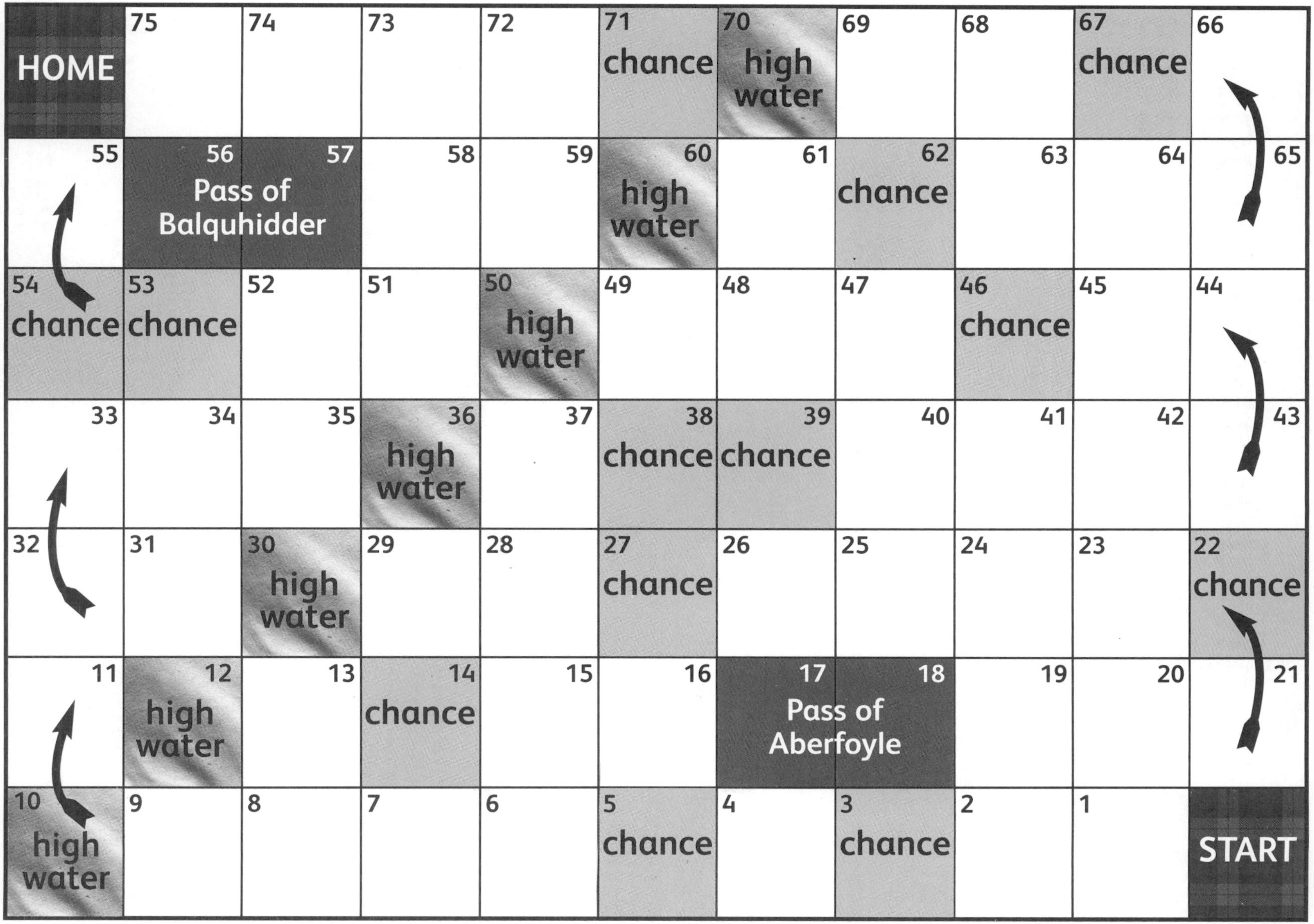

HOME
75
74
73
72
71 chance
70 high water
69
68
67 chance
66
55
56 57 Pass of Balquhidder
58
59
60 high water
61
62 chance
63
64
65
54 chance
53 chance
52
51
50 high water
49
48
47
46 chance
45
44
33
34
35
36 high water
37
38 chance
39 chance
40
41
42
43
32
31
30 high water
29
28
27 chance
26
25
24
23
22 chance
11
12 high water
13
14 chance
15
16
17 18 Pass of Aberfoyle
19
20
21
10 high water
9
8
7
6
5 chance
4
3 chance
2
1
START

Jacobite songs and story-poems

From BONNIE DUNDEE

To the Lords of Convention 'twas Claver'se who spoke:
'Ere the king's crown shall fall there are crowns to be
   broke;
So let each cavalier who loves honour and me,
Come follow the bonnet of Bonnie Dundee!'

Dundee he is mounted, he rides up the street,
The bells are rung backward, the drums they are beat;
But the Provost, douce man, said, 'Just e'en let him be,
The gude town is weel quit of that deil of Dundee.'

He spurred to the foot of the proud Castle rock,
And with the gay Gordon he gallantly spoke:
'Let Mons Meg and her marrows speak twa words or
   three,
For the love of the bonnet of Bonnie Dundee.

'There are hills beyond Pentlands, and lands beyond
   Forth;
If there's lords in the Lowlands, there's chiefs in the
   north;
There are wild Duniewassals three thousand times
   three,
Will cry, "Hoigh, for the bonnets of Bonnie Dundee!"'

He waved his proud hand, and the trumpets were
   blown,
The kettle-drums clashed, and the horsemen rode on,
Till on Ravelston's cliffs and on Clermiston's lee,
Died away the wild war notes of Bonnie Dundee.

   Come fill up my cup, come fill up my can,
   Come saddle the horses, and call out the men;
   Come open your gates and let me gae free,
   For it's up with the bonnets of Bonnie Dundee.

                        Sir Walter Scott (1771-1832)

– douce = sober, respectable / deil = devil
– Mons Meg: huge cannon, made in the 15th century and weighing
   about six tons, which can still be seen at Edinburgh Castle; it was
   last fired to celebrate the birthday of the future James VII in 1681,
   when it burst.
– marrows = comrades / Duniewassals = clansmen

From THE BURIAL-MARCH OF DUNDEE

Down we crouched amid the bracken,
   Till the Lowland ranks drew near,
Panting like the hounds in summer,
   When they scent the stately deer.
From the dark defile emerging,
   Next we saw the squadrons come,
Leslie's foot and Leven's troopers
   Marching to the tuck of drum.
Through the scattered wood of birches,
   O'er the broken ground and heath,
Wound the long battalion slowly,
   Till they gained the plain beneath;
Then we bounded from our covert –
   Judge how looked the Saxon then,
When they saw the rugged mountain
   Start to life with armed men!
Like a tempest down the ridges
   Swept the hurricane of steel,
Rose the slogan of Macdonald –
   Flashed the broadsword of Lochiel!
Vainly sped the withering volley
   'Mongst the foremost of our band –
On we poured until we met them,
   Foot to foot, and hand to hand.
Horse and man went down like drift-wood
   When the floods are black at Yule,
And their carcasses are whirling
   In the Garry's deepest pool.
Horse and man went down before us –
   Living foe there tarried none
On the field of Killiecrankie,
   When that stubborn fight was done.

                        William Edmonstoune Aytoun (1813-65)

IT WAS A' FOR OUR RIGHTFU' KING

It was a' for our rightfu' king
    We left fair Scotland's strand;
It was a' for our rightfu' king,
    We e'er saw Irish land,
        My dear –
    We e'er saw Irish land.

Now a' is done that men can do,
    And a' is done in vain,
My Love and Native Land fareweel,
    For I maun cross the main,
        My dear –
    For I maun cross the main.

He turn'd him right and round about
    Upon the Irish shore,
And gae his bridle reins a shake,
    With adieu for ever more,
        My dear –
    And adieu for ever more.

The soger from the wars returns,
    The sailor from the main,
But I hae parted frae my love
    Never to meet again,
        My dear –
    Never to meet again.

When day is gane, and night is come,
    And a' folk bound to sleep,
I think on him that's far awa
    The lee-lang night, and weep,
        My dear –
    The lee-lang night and weep.

Robert Burns (1759-96)

– In 1689, James VII landed in Ireland, where he took office as king,
  with an Irish parliament, and a Catholic army to defend him. He
  was defeated by King William at the battle of the Boyne, and once
  again fled to France. The first two and the fourth verses of this
  song are spoken by one of James' military staff, forced into exile
  with his king; his love in Scotland speaks the last.
– maun = must / lee-lang = livelong

From THE BATTLE OF SHERIFFMUIR

There's some say that we wan,
    And some say that they wan,
And some say that nane wan at 'a, man;
    But one thing I'm sure, that at Sherramuir,
A battle there was that I saw, man.
    And we ran, and they ran, and they ran, and we ran,
    But Florence was fastest of a', man.

– Florence was the name of the horse of the Marquis of Huntly, one
  of the Jacobite cavalry commanders at Sheriffmuir.

From the ballad of LORD DERWENTWATER

King George has written a long letter,
    And sealed it o'er with gold,
And sent it to Lord Derwentwater,
    To read it if he would.

The very first line that my lord did read,
    He gave a smirkling smile;
The very next line that he looked upon,
    The tears from his eyes did fall.

'Come saddle to me my horse,' he said,
    'Come saddle to me with speed.
For I must away to London town,
    To answer for my head.'

They had not rode a mile but one,
    Till his horse fell o'er a stone:
'It's warning good enough,' he said,
    'Alive I'll ne'er come home!'

When they came to fair London town,
    Into the courtiers' hall,
The lords and knights of London town
    Did him a traitor call.

'A traitor! A traitor!' says my lord,
    'A traitor, how can that be?
Unless for keeping five hundred men
    To fight for King Jamie.

'All lords and knights in London town,
    Come out and see me die;
You lords and knights of London town,
    Be kind to my lady.

'There's fifty pounds in my right pocket,
    Divide it to the poor;
There's fifty and four in my left pocket,
    Divide it from door to door.'

CHARLIE HE'S MY DARLING

'Twas on a Monday morning,
    Right early in the year,
That Charlie came to our town,
    The young Chevalier.
        And Charlie he's my darling,
        My darling, my darling,
        And Charlie he's my darling,
        The young Chevalier.

As he was walking up the street,
    The city for to view,
O there he spied a bonny lass,
    The window looking through.
        And Charlie he's my darling, etc.

Sae light's he jumped up the stair,
    And tirled at the pin;
And wha sae ready as herself
    To let the laddie in!
        And Charlie he's my darling, etc.

He set his Jenny on his knee,
    All in his Highland dress;
For brawly well he kend the way
    To please a bonny lass.
        And Charlie he's my darling, etc.

It's up yon heathery mountain,
    And down yon scroggy glen,
We daurna gang a-milking
    For Charlie and his men.
        And Charlie he's my darling,
        My darling, my darling,
        And Charlie he's my darling,
        The young Chevalier.

Robert Burns (1759-96)

JOHNNIE COPE

Cope sent a letter frae Dunbar:
'Charlie, meet me an ye daur,
And I'll learn you the art o' war,
    If you'll meet me in the morning.'

        Hey, Johnny Cope, are ye wauking yet?
        Or are your drums a-beating yet?
        If ye were wauking I wad wait
            To gang to the coals i' the morning.

When Charlie looked the letter upon,
He drew his sword the scabbard from:
'Come, follow me, my merry merry men,
    And we'll meet Johnnie Cope in the morning!

'Now, Johnnie, be as good's your word;
Come, let us try both fire and sword;
And dinna flee away like a frighted bird,
    That's chased frae its nest in the morning.'

When Johnnie Cope he heard o' this
He thought it wadna be amiss
To ha'e a horse in readiness
    To flee awa' in the morning.

Fye now, Johnnie get up and rin;
The Highland bagpipes mak' a din;
It's best to sleep in a hale skin,
    For 'twill be a bluidy morning.

When Johnnie Cope to Dunbar came
They speered at him, 'Where's a' your men?'
'The deil confound me gin I ken,
    For I left them a' in the morning.'

Now, Johnnie, troth, ye are na blate
To come wi' the news o' your ain defeat,

And leave your men in sic a strait
    Sae early in the morning.

'Oh, faith,' quo' Johnnie, 'I got sic flegs
Wi' their claymores and philabegs;
If I face them again, deil break my legs!
    So I wish you a gude morning.'

Adam Skirving (1719-1803)

– speered = asked / blate = bashful / fleg = fright

Dumfounder'd, they heard the blaw, the blaw,
Dumfounder'd, they ran awa', awa',
From the hundred pipers an' a', an' a'.
    Wi' a hundred pipers an' a', an' a',
    Wi' a hundred pipers an' a', an' a',
    We'll up and gie them a blaw, a blaw,
    Wi' a hundred pipers an' a', an' a'.

Lady Nairne (1766-1845)

– fu' wae = very woeful / grat = wept / maist = almost /
unco flare = surprising blast

THE HUNDRED PIPERS

Wi' a hundred pipers an' a', an' a',
Wi' a hundred pipers an' a', an' a';
We'll up an' gie them a blaw, a blaw,
Wi' a hundred pipers an' a', an' a.
Oh, it's owre the Border awa', awa',
It's owre the Border awa', awa',
We'll on and we'll march to Carlisle ha',
Wi' its yetts, its castell, an' a', an' a'.

Oh, our sodger lads looked braw, looked braw,
Wi' their tartans, kilts, an' a', an' a',
Wi' their bonnets, an' feathers, an' glittering gear,
An' pibrochs sounding sweet and clear.
Will they a' return, our Hieland men?
Second-sighted Sandy looked fu' wae,
And mothers grat when they marched away.
    Wi' a hundred pipers, etc.

Oh, wha is foremost o' a', o' a'?
Oh, wha does follow the blaw, the blaw?
Bonnie Charlie, the king o' us a', hurra',
Wi' his hundred pipers an' a', an' a'.
His bonnet an' feather, he's wavin' high,
His prancing steed maist seems to fly,
The nor' wind plays wi' his curly hair,
While the pipers blaw in an unco
    flare.
    Wi' a hundred pipers, etc.

The Esk was swollen, sae red and sae
    deep,
But shouther to shouther the brave lads
    keep;
Twa thousand swam owre to fell English
    ground,
An' danced themselves dry to the pibroch's
    sound.
Dumfounder'd, the English saw – they saw –

THE LOVELY LASS O' INVERNESS

The lovely lass o' Inverness,
    Nae joy nor pleasure she can see;
For e'en and morn she cries, 'Alas!'
    And aye the saut tear blinds her e'e.
'Drummossie Moor! Drummossie day!
    A waefu' day it was to me;
For there I lost my father dear,
    My father dear, and brethren three.

'Their winding-sheet's the bluidy clay,
    Their graves are growing green to see;
And by them lies the dearest lad
    That ever blest a woman's e'e.
Now wae to thee, thou cruel lord!
    A bluidy man I trow thou be;
For many a heart thou hast made sair,
    That ne'er did wrong to thine or thee.'

WILL YE NO COME BACK AGAIN?

Bonnie Chairlie's noo awa',
    Safely owre the friendly main;
    Mony a heart will break in twa',
    Should he ne'er come back again.
    Will ye no come back again?
Will ye no come back again?
Better lo'ed ye canna be,
Will ye no come back again?

Ye trusted in your Hielan' men,
    They trusted you dear Chairlie.
They kent your hidin' in the glen,
    Death or exile bravin'.
    Will ye no come back again, etc.

We watched thee in the gloamin' hour,
We watched thee in the mornin' grey.
Tho' thirty thousand pounds they gie,
O there is nane that wad betray.
  , Will ye no' come back again, etc.

Sweet the laverock's note and lang,
Liltin' wildly up the glen.
But aye tae me he sings ae sang,

Will ye no come back again?
   Will ye no come back again?
   Will ye no come back again?
   Better lo'ed ye canna be,
   Will ye no come back again?

Lady Nairne (1766-1845)

— kent = knew / laverock = skylark

ANSWERS TO JACOBITES' QUIZ

(1) True. She is also descended from Robert the Bruce through her mother's family of Bowes-Lyon, whose founder, Sir John Lyon of Glamis, married Princess Joanna, daughter of Robert II.

(2) The royal line of the Stewarts began with Marjorie, daughter of Robert the Bruce, and ended with Queen Anne, who had no children who survived. His prophecy, therefore, was true.

(3) c.   (4)   b.

(5) False. There were no clan tartans at this time.

(6) True.   (7) c, d, e, f.   (8) b.   (9) b.

(10) True. He chose the wrong ground, his soldiers were tired out, and he delayed the order to charge, which resulted in heavy casualties.

(11) a/C, b/D, c/E, d/B, e/F, f/A.

FURTHER CREDITS

CASSELL'S *OLD AND NEW EDINBURGH: Its History, its People, and its Places* by James Grant (Cassell & Co.: London, no date) – for pages 8 (High Street, Edinburgh); 22 (Charles Edward Stuart); activities section page i (Charles Edward Stuart)

THE COMPREHENSIVE HISTORY OF ENGLAND: Civil, Military, Religious, Intellectual and Social by Macfarlane and Thomson (Blackie & Son: Glasgow, no date) – for pages 2-3 (James VI/I, Anne, George IV); 5 (William and Mary); 14 (George I); activities section page i (William III, James Edward Stuart, George IV); vi (Cope signature); vi (Charles Edward Stuart)

A HISTORY OF THE SCOTTISH HIGHLANDS, HIGHLAND CLANS AND HIGHLAND REGIMENTS, Kelty (ed.) (Fullarton: Edinburgh, 1877) – for p. 9 and activities section p. i (Cameron of Lochiel) (loaned by Inverness Library, The Highland Council [LSU])

MEMORIALS OF EDINBURGH IN THE OLDEN TIME, D. Wilson (vol. 1) (Hugh Paton: Edinburgh, 1848) – for page 25 (Netherbow)

BLAIR CASTLE, PERTHSHIRE (© From the Collection at Blair Castle, Perthshire) – pages 21 (John Murray, 1st Duke of Atholl); 24 (George Murray)

BLAIR TRUST MUSEUM (© Trustees of the Blair Museum. Licensor www.scran.ac.uk) – for page 37 (Charles Edward Stuart [above, right])

EWAN STEEL – for pages 6 (figures putting on plaid); 16 (Sheriff-muir battle plan); 23 (clan insignia x 5)

NATIONAL GALLERIES OF SCOTLAND
SCOTTISH NATIONAL PORTRAIT GALLERY – for pages 4 (*Prince James Francis Edward Stuart 1688-1766*, by unknown artist [detail]); 5 (*Prince Charles Edward Stuart 1720-1788*, by Antonio David [detail]); 8 (John Graham of Claverhouse, Viscount Dundee 1648-1689, by David Paton [detail]); 17 (*James Drummond, 2nd Duke of Perth 1673-1720*, by Sir John Baptiste de Medina [detail]); 19 (*The Solemnization of the Marriage of Prince James Francis Edward Stewart and Princess Maria Clementina*, by Agustino Masucci); 19 (*Field-Marshal George Wade, 1673-1748*, by Johan van Deist); 34 (*Flora MacDonald*, by Richard Wilson [detail]); 35 (*Prince Charles Edward Stuart dressed as Betty Burke*, by J. Williams); 37 (*Prince Charles Edward Stuart 1720-1788*, by Maurice Quentin de la Tour [detail]); 37 (*Princess Louisa of Stolberg, 1753-1824*, by unknown artist [detail]); 37 (*Clementina Walkinshaw*, unknown artist [detail]); 37 (*Charlotte Stewart*, Hugh Douglas Hamilton [detail])

NATIONAL LIBRARY OF SCOTLAND (© The Trustees of the National Library of Scotland) – for pages 9 (*The Prospect of Edinburgh from Ye Dean 1693*, EMS.b.5.1); 13 (*Order for the Glencoe Massacre*, Adv. Ms. 23.6.24); 23 (*Charles Prince of Wales proclamation …, 1745*, DOD 74970677/79); 35 (*The Lyon in Mourning*, Adv. Mss. 32.6.16-32.6.26; 38 (*The America, A Collection of Scotch Airs* [David Young], 1740, Mss. 2084-2085); 39 (George IV Visit to Scotland, [G. Cruikshank etching], *Lond. 1822*, Ry.1.1.179)

NATIONAL MUSEUMS SCOTLAND
With thanks to George Dalgleish and Jonathan Ferguson for advice and assistance.

NATIONAL PORTRAIT GALLERY (© National Portrait Gallery, London) – for page 15 (*John Campbell, 2nd Duke of Argyll and Duke of Greenwich*, by William Aikman)

THE NATIONAL TRUST FOR SCOTLAND (Reproduced by kind permission of The National Trust for Scotland) – for pages 11 (*The Battle of Killiecrankie*, by Alan B. Heriot; John Dalrymple, 1st Earl of Stair [National Trust for Scotland/John Sinclair]); 22 (*Action at Sea*, by Harold Wylie); 30 (Culloden re-enactment [National Trust for Scotland/Immersion Filming])

PENICUIK DRAWINGS (© The Penicuik Drawings are reproduced with the kind permission of Sir Robert Clerk Bt. of Penicuik) – for pages 27 (Highlanders x 3); 29 (Jacobite Hussar)

UNIVERSITY OF STIRLING ARCHIVES (© Amulree Collection of Jacobite Material, formerly Lumisden-Strange Collection) – for page 37 (*Prince Charles Edward Stuart* by Hugh Douglas Hamilton [below, right])